MINIATURE ROSES

MINIATURE ROSES

AN ILLUSTRATED GUIDE TO VARIETIES, CULTIVATION AND CARE, WITH
STEP-BY-STEP INSTRUCTIONS AND OVER 145 GLORIOUS PHOTOGRAPHS

Lin Hawthorne

Photography by Peter Anderson

southwater

This edition is published by Southwater
an imprint of Anness Publishing Ltd
108 Great Russell Street, London WC1B 3NA
info@anness.com

www.southwaterbooks.com; www.annesspublishing.com

If you like the images in this book and would like to investigate
using them for publishing, promotions or advertising, please visit
our website www.practicalpictures.com for more information.

© Anness Publishing Ltd 2014

A CIP catalogue record for this book is available from the British Library.

Publisher: Joanna Lorenz
Editor: Margaret Malone
Designer: Kathryn Gammon
Production Controller: Pirong Wang

PUBLISHER'S NOTE
Although the advice and information in this book are believed to be accurate and true at the time
of going to press, neither the authors nor the publisher can accept any legal responsibility or liability
for any errors or omissions that may have been made nor for any inaccuracies nor for any loss,
harm or injury that comes about from following instructions or advice in this book.

■ HALF TITLE PAGE
'White Cécile Brünner'
■ FRONTISPIECE
'Hakuun'
■ TITLE PAGE
Large-flowered hybrid tea

■ LEFT
'Laura Ford'
■ OPPOSITE LEFT
'Crimson Gem'
■ OPPOSITE RIGHT
'Sweet Magic'

Contents

INTRODUCTION

What is a rose? *8*

The history of miniature roses *10*

Using small roses in the garden *12*

Miniature roses in the home *17*

Classification of roses *18*

PLANT DIRECTORY *20*

THE GROWER'S GUIDE

Buying miniature roses *40*

Planting and growing
miniature roses *42*

Planting in open ground *44*

Planting in containers *46*

Planting in a hanging basket *48*

Pegging down ground-cover roses *49*

Care and maintenance *50*

Propagation *52*

Pruning *56*

Calendar *57*

Pests and diseases *58*

Other recommended roses *60*

Index *64*

Introduction

*A*t one time a rose garden was the prerogative of gardeners with masses of space to devote to the culture of one of the world's favourite flowers. In today's smaller modern gardens, where space is inevitably restricted, it is difficult to select just one or two of the larger roses from the thousands of beautiful varieties available. However, the advent of miniature and Patio roses has caused a revolution in rose-growing. Their versatility and compact size, combined with their ability to produce an abundance of beautiful blooms over very long periods – often almost continuously from summer to the first frosts of autumn – has brought the joys of rose-growing to gardeners with even the tiniest of plots. In future years, the gardening world will, no doubt, welcome many more introductions of these lovely little roses.

■ RIGHT
Diminutive roses, such as the delicate 'Little White Pet', bring grace and beauty to even the smallest of plots.

What is a rose?

The genus Rosa comprises some 150 species of evergreen and deciduous shrubs and climbers, as well as many thousands of hybrid cultivars developed from the species over many centuries. The rose has been known in cultivation since humankind first gardened, so it should not be surprising that there are roses to suit almost every climate and situation.

Roses occur naturally in a wide range of habitats, from sea-level to subalpine altitudes, in seaside dunes, open scrubland, hedgerows and woodland, where rambling roses scramble through forest trees in their quest for light and warmth. They range over the world's continents from North America to Asia and from Europe to North Africa.

In the wild, the majority of these roses bloom only once, usually in one glorious and frequently spectacular summer flush, followed by the hips or fruits that guarantee the next generation. But over the centuries, rose breeders have succeeded in creating not only plants that produce more and better flowers, but also many willing, hard-working shrubs that display their flowers repeatedly or continuously over very many months – a feature that simply cannot be equalled by any other single group of shrubs.

The beauty of roses

Roses vary in size from the tiniest miniatures, no more than 25cm (10in) in height, to massive sprawling ramblers that may achieve 30m (100ft) if left to their own devices. Almost without exception, they are valued for their beautiful, often richly

■ ABOVE
Rosa 'Yellow Flower Carpet', a ground-cover rose.

■ RIGHT
The silky, many-petalled flowers of a shrub rose.

■ RIGHT
The large-flowered bush roses (Hybrid Teas) are renowned for the perfection of their urn-shaped flowers.

fragrant blooms, and many also have foliage that is attractive in its own right, as well as providing an admirable foil for the flowers.

Their flowers are also diverse, from the beautiful simplicity of the single-flowered wild dog rose, *Rosa canina*, whose five-petalled flowers open flat to reveal a boss of golden stamens, through to the many-petalled Chinquapin rose, *Rosa roxburghii*. The breeder's art has given us many other flower forms, some simple and still recognizably near those of the species, others very

densely packed with silken petals. There are the perfect urn-shaped flowers of the large-flowered bush roses (Hybrid Teas) – such as those of the famous 'Peace' – which open from the high-pointed buds, and the many-petalled Floribundas. Add to these the rosettes (some of which have petals that are arranged in 'quarters') and pompons, and you have some idea of their great variety.

Roses also offer an extraordinary diversity of habitat: they may be open and upright or gracefully arching shrubs; dense, thicket-forming, thorny bushes; or rampant trailing and scrambling ramblers and climbers. In this book, we are primarily concerned with those examples of the genus which, either

■ ABOVE
Rosa 'Peace', one of the most famous of modern Hybrid Teas.

by accident or design, are small and thus easily accommodated within the confines of the small modern garden. That is not to say that miniature roses do not have a place in grander gardens, but one of their indubitable advantages is that they offer colour and sometimes fragrance to those who can aspire to little more than a flower-filled balcony or courtyard. We have not restricted ourselves to the true miniatures – little bushes of about 25m (10in) tall, which were originally used as pot plants. The plants described here also include the smaller examples from other modern groups, the Patio roses and ground-cover roses, as well as the older, diminutive varieties from the China, Polyantha and Centifolia roses.

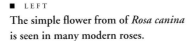
■ LEFT
The simple flower from of *Rosa canina* is seen in many modern roses.

The history of miniature roses

Until the end of the 17th century, nearly all of the roses grown in European gardens flowered once only, around mid-summer. These are some of the most ancient roses: the Albas, Gallicas, Damasks and Centifolias, along with their mossy sports, the Moss roses. Many are still grown and are much loved to this day for their pure colours and heavenly fragrance. But the introduction of *Rosa chinensis*, the China rose, revolutionized rose breeding in Europe, for it is this species and its variants that possessed the invaluable characteristic of 'remontancy', or repeat-flowering.

In 1781, a pink-flowered China rose known as 'Old Blush China' (now known as *R. × odorata* 'Pallida') was introduced to the Netherlands from India. Several years later, the British East India Company brought the crimson-flowered *R. semperflorens* or 'Slater's Crimson China' to Britain. The importance of these plants in rose breeding can hardly be overestimated. The genetic legacy of these two Chinese roses is expressed in almost all of the roses that flower repeatedly today.

In the early years, the Chinese roses were crossed with European roses to yield the repeat-flowering Bourbons,

■ ABOVE

Rosa 'Old Blush China' was one of the most important introductions, bringing repeat-flowering genes to modern roses.

Portlands, Noisettes and Tea roses and, finally, the Hybrid Perpetuals, the elegant forerunners of the modern Hybrid Teas (now called large-flowered bush roses). The era of the modern rose began in 1867 with the introduction of the first Hybrid Tea, 'La France', which was probably as a result of a chance cross between a Hybrid Perpetual and a Tea rose.

Further developments followed rapidly. By introducing the genes of *R. moschata* and *R. multiflora* to those of *R. chinensis*, a new, very hardy race – the dwarf Polyanthas – eventually emerged around 1900.

■ OPPOSITE LEFT
Rosa 'Rouletii', syn. *R. chinensis* var.
minima, also known as the Pygmy rose.

■ RIGHT
Rosa 'White
Flower Carpet'
produces clusters
of small, double,
lightly scented,
white flowers
from summer
to autumn.

These were first developed by the Poulsen nurseries in Denmark. The eventual result was the Floribundas, or cluster-flowered bush roses.

It is worth bearing in mind the origin of these roses. To be so successful in the harsh winter climates of continental and northern Europe, these compact and floriferous bushes needed to be extremely tough and hardy. Again, this constitutional legacy is one that benefits growers of modern roses; their descendants, the dwarf cluster-flowered bushes, better known as 'Patio roses', are very cold-tolerant. Most derive from crossings of Floribundas with dwarf Polyanthas and miniature roses. Their group name is somewhat unfortunate, for although they are undoubtedly of suitable proportions for growing in pots to decorate a patio, it scarcely describes their versatility in gardens.

Origins of miniature roses

The origins of the true miniature roses are still mysterious, although many experts agree that the original miniatures were probably diminutive sports (mutations) of a China rose; indeed, *R. chinensis* seems, throughout its long history, to have proved a particularly valuable species. After its

introduction to Europe, the earliest miniatures appear to have been grown primarily as houseplants. What is certain is that the discovery, by a Swiss army officer named Roulet in 1918, of tiny roses of this type decorating the window ledges of Swiss chalets stimulated the interest of Dutch and Spanish hybridizers. The genes of *Rosa* 'Rouletii' (syn. *R. chinensis* var. *minima,* now known as 'Pompon de Paris') are obviously present in many of the modern miniatures grown in gardens today.

The 1980s saw the advent of a new rose revolution: the creation of the so-called ground-cover roses that would reduce the need for weeding by shading out some weeds with their dense-leaved habit. Again, the term

'ground-cover' does little justice to their versatility.

The development of the ground-cover roses and miniature roses has continued apace in the UK, in continental Europe and, especially for the miniatures, in the United States. Given this provenance, you can be sure that these roses will be cold-hardy in all but the most severe of climates. The increase in popularity of these small roses went hand-in-hand with the general reduction in the size of gardens in the latter part of the 20th century. Having found a considerable market demand, there is no doubt that their ranks will swell in future years. As yet, there are relatively few miniature climbers, but breeders are working hard on the case.

Using small roses in the garden

For many years we became used
to seeing beds and borders filled
exclusively with roses in serried,
formal ranks, emerging stiffly upright
above sterile areas of bare soil.
Indeed, many rose growers still regard
this as the 'correct' way to grow
them. While the formal rose bed
still undoubtedly has its place, it is
increasingly difficult not to view
this treatment of roses as singularly
lacking in imagination, given the
diversity of size, habit and flowering
period of roses as a group. The new
roses, especially the smaller-growing
ones, prove exceptionally versatile,
and their uses in gardens are limited
only by the imagination of the grower
and the chosen style of garden.

■ ABOVE
Tightly packed clusters of flowers
are typical of the Patio roses.

■ BELOW LEFT
A low ribbon of roses flanking a path
draws the eye to an elegant focal point.

Miniature roses

Ranging in height from the tiniest,
such as Rosa 'Rouletii' at 12cm (5in)
tall, to the general run of miniatures
at around 25–40cm (10–16in)
in height, perhaps the primary
consideration when using miniatures
is that they should be placed where
they can be appreciated at close
quarters. While the larger cultivars
can be put to much the same uses as
the Patio roses, the smallest ones are
at their best in containers that bring

■ RIGHT
Ground-cover roses cascade over the edge of a raised bed. Raised beds allow miniature roses to be brought closer to eye level.

them up to, or very nearly up to, eye level. They are perfect in pots, troughs and window boxes, and they are even tough enough to be grown on high balconies in this way. Miniatures are also very useful for hanging baskets, either on their own or in mixed plantings with trailing annuals, such as lobelia, or the long, cascading stems of *Helichrysum petiolare* (syn. *H. petiolatum*), with its soft, sage-grey leaves. They are equally at home in small raised beds, which is a particularly valuable way of growing them in small courtyard gardens, where open areas of soil are absent or at a premium. Some growers use miniatures in the rock garden. While their scale suits this type of site, they can be difficult to place there, since their highly bred style seldom associates well with alpine plants, which have a more natural habit of growth.

Many older cultivars were originally used as pot plants for decorating the home. Indeed, their revival in popularity has seen increased sales of miniatures as houseplants in supermarkets and garden centres, although the choice here is often fairly limited and they are seldom sold as named varieties. While their colour and diminutive beauty can clearly be appreciated at close quarters

when grown as houseplants, if they are to achieve any degree of permanence, they must have excellent light. Most perform best if given periodic spells in a well-lit conservatory, or if moved to a sunny spot outdoors during the summer months.

Patio roses

Dwarf cluster-flowered roses, popularly known as Patio roses, are neat, compact little bushes, which are usually covered in wide clusters of flowers throughout the summer, until stopped by the first hard frosts of autumn. With most in the size range of 40–75cm (16–30in) tall by as much across, these small, free-flowering bushes earn their keep in even the

tiniest sites. The term 'Patio rose' suggests unjustified restrictions on their use. They are, indeed, ideal for planting in terracotta pots, tubs and urns, and they will provide many months of pleasure when they are placed on patios, balconies and terraces and in porches, but they have a range of other uses, too.

Patio roses are often used as massed bedding in a formal bed or border, and this is an ideal way of growing them if solid blocks of long-lasting colour are needed. Most have the advantages of hardiness and a healthy constitution, which is important in massed plantings, where uniformity of colour and performance is an absolute requirement. This uniformity can

Trailing ground-cover roses, grown as weeping standards, can be trained both to decorate a hedge and frame an entrance.

■ ABOVE
Roses do not need to be trailing to be effective in hanging baskets, as these ground-cover roses demonstrate.

also be put to good use when they are planted as low hedging or as edging to a border or pathway.

When grown as a single or double row flanking a path, they provide a low, continuous ribbon of colour that is beautiful in its own right. They also perform an invaluable design function by drawing the eye along the planting scheme, which may then terminate in an attractive focal point, such as a rose arch, statue or tall, elegant container, where climbing roses can continue the theme.

Ground-cover roses

These are among the most versatile of the smaller roses, especially the repeat-flowering cultivars of more modern breeding. Ground-cover roses come in two main types, both equally hardy: the compact, very bushy and slightly spreading types, such as 'Laura Ashley' (syn. 'Chewharia'); and the trailing ground-cover roses, such as 'Nozomi' (syn. 'Heideröslein'), which have long, flexible stems that root where they touch the ground.

The spreading growth tends to form a low mound of foliage that is perfect for the front of a shrub or mixed border, mixing well with shrubs and perennials.

Ground-cover roses, especially the trailing sorts, are perfect for clothing sunny banks, especially those that are awkward and inaccessible, since most require little maintenance or pruning. Their trailing habit is displayed to great advantage if allowed to cascade from a height: each flexible stem will be wreathed along its entire length with bloom for much of the summer.

They can be grown over retaining walls or from the top of a terrace, planted in tall pots and urns, or in large, moss-lined hanging baskets. Many are also available as standards, grafted on to the top of a long, straight stem to give a graceful, weeping effect. Moreover, if you use them in any of these ways where they can be reflected in still water, you double their beauty instantly.

Their effectiveness as ground cover relies on the density of their foliage to exclude light and so reduce weed growth beneath them. Since many are deciduous, some experts consider 'ground-cover' a misleading term, for the growth of some weed species continues unabated during the cold months, when the roses are leafless. If they are to be effective as ground cover, thorough preparation in advance is absolutely fundamental to their success.

They must be planted in very clean, weed-free soil and top-dressed with a weed suppressant mulch, such as chipped bark, or planted through a sheet mulch of landscaping fabric.

■ RIGHT
In this cottage garden, roses blend perfectly with love-in-a-mist (*Nigella damascena*).

Dwarf Polyanthas, Chinas and Centifolias

The small bushes in this group often have a graceful habit, with airy sprays of bloom that associate particularly well with herbaceous perennials and with other shrubs in a mixed border. They are ideal for cottage-garden style plantings, and their restricted height makes them particularly suitable for low hedging, useful when you need to create barriers between different parts of the garden. They also make ideal

container plants, with an elegant habit that suits a range of pots, tubs and urns. Use them to decorate a patio or courtyard, to create a focal point or to mark a change in style or level within the garden. Alternatively, pairs can be used to flank an entrance.

Most of this group of small roses, which includes the Polyantha 'Cécile Brünner' (syn. 'Mignon', 'Sweetheart Rose') and its sport 'Perle d'Or' (syn. 'Yellow Cécile Brünner'), have been grown in gardens for over a century, and are hardy and reliable.

Miniature climbers

In small gardens, where space is inevitably restricted, these climbers, which seldom grow to more than 2.1m (7ft) tall and 1.2m (4ft) across, are perfect for clothing walls or fences, either to form a feature in their own right or to be a backdrop for other foreground plantings. Grown against a wall or on free-standing architectural structures, such as pyramids or tripods, they provide a strong vertical element in a design.

Most miniature climbers flower almost continuously throughout summer and have the advantage of remaining well clothed with foliage almost down to ground level. This is seldom true of large climbers, which tend to become bare at the base unless they are trained firmly to the horizontal during their early years.

In courtyards, where soil beds are impracticable for reasons of space, miniature climbers can be grown in large pots or tubs. As with all types of container cultivation, however, easy access to a water source is essential. Plants in pots dry out rapidly in hot weather, especially if warm, dry conditions are prolonged, and you need to check them daily.

■ ABOVE
The elegant rose garden at Chatsworth, in Derbyshire, England, complete with formal clipped hedges and pillars clothed in magnificent climbing roses.

■ LEFT
A miniature climber looks charming twining up a rustic wooden support.

Miniature roses in the home

Miniature and small roses are perfect for cutting and using in posies and other diminutive arrangements. They last best if cut early in the day, because then the stems are turgid (full of water). Leave as long a length of stem as possible, remove the lowest leaves and thorns, and plunge them up to their necks in cold water for a few hours before arranging. Immediately before arranging, trim the stem with a slanting cut while still under water. You may need to provide the support of florists' foam, wire mesh or a scrunch of wire netting for arrangements.

Roses of most colours blend well with shades of blue, as provided by the spires of delphiniums, or for a cottage-garden style, by scabious, nigella, cornflowers, or larkspur. Gypsophila, with its airy panicles of

small white flowers, adds an element of textural contrast. Flowers in the apricot-pink to salmon band of the spectrum look particularly good against bronze or purple foliage, such as that of copper beech, *Fagus sylvatica f. purpurea*, or *Cotinus coggygria*. Those in the clear pink and

crimson-red range are set off perfectly against the silver-grey leaves of plants like the artemisias and lavenders.

When growing miniatures as pot plants, use a loam-based mix (such as John Innes No. 2 or a commercially prepared planting mix), and provide bright light but avoid exposure to hot midday sun through glass, which may scorch the plant. Keep evenly moist and feed with a balanced fertilizer at two- to three-week intervals throughout the growing season. Indoor roses suffer from lack of light, and may eventually cease to grow and flower well, but during the summer months they can be moved outdoors or transferred to a site with high light levels, such as a conservatory. Prune and deadhead as for outdoor roses.

■ TOP LEFT
AND RIGHT
Very versatile, miniature roses are at home in dried arrangements in containers.

■ RIGHT
Plunge freshly cut roses up to their necks in cool fresh water for a few hours.

Classification of roses

Over the centuries, hybridization has made the botanical classification of roses complex. It is more useful to the gardener to group them by growth and flowering habit – some groups are better suited to certain garden uses than others. To this end, the world's rose societies have developed a horticultural classification thus:

Wild or species roses

Wild roses and hybrids with features that clearly identify them as offspring of a particular species. They include shrubs, ramblers and climbers, most blooming only once but with the additional interest of colourful hips.

Old garden roses

With few exceptions, these are once-blooming roses; they include Albas, Gallicas, Damasks, Centifolias and Moss roses, along with Scotch roses, derived from *R. pimpinellifolia*, and Sweet Briars, from *R. eglanteria*. There are shrubs of varied size and habit, with a range of flower shapes and colours, many intensely fragrant. Most are too large to be included here, but there are a few diminutive Centifolias, such as 'De Meaux' and 'Petite de Hollande'.

Early hybrids of European and Oriental roses

Mostly repeat-flowering roses derived from crossings with *R. chinensis*. They include Chinas, Portlands, Noisettes, Bourbons, Tea and Hybrid Perpetual roses. With the exception of a few dainty China roses, such as 'Comtesse du Cayla' and 'Fabvier', the majority of these roses are too large to belong in this book.

Modern roses

The development of reliably repeat-flowering roses spawned a whole new generation, and it is within this broad grouping of 'Modern Roses' that

ROSE FLOWER FORMS

As detailed opposite, there are a number of descriptive terms covering the distinctive forms of rose flowers. These can be a useful guide, though in reality many fall somewhere between the types. They are also grouped by number of petals, as follows:
- Single: 8 or fewer petals
- Semi-double: 8–20 petals
- Double: 20 or more petals
- Fully double: over 30 petals

■ ABOVE

Flat, single

most of the small roses belong. Here, we find the large-flowered bush roses (Hybrid Teas), the cluster-flowered bush roses (Floribundas), the climbers and ramblers, and modern shrubs such as the Rugosas. Within this overall classification, the groups that most concern us here are as follows:

Polyanthas – Compact, very hardy, relatively thornless shrubs and climbers, with small leaves and sprays of small, single to double flowers. All are repeat-flowering, to a greater or lesser degree, most varieties blooming in several flushes, lasting from early summer to autumn, rather than continuously.

Patio roses – Diminutive versions of Floribundas, Patio roses are also known as dwarf cluster-flowered bushes. Compact bushes with usually glossy leaves and single or double blooms in clusters from summer to autumn. All are hardy, and most show good disease-resistance.

■ ABOVE

Cupped, double

■ ABOVE

Rosette-shaped, double

■ ABOVE

Quartered-rosette, fully double

Ground-cover roses – Low-growing, spreading or trailing, often prickly roses with clusters of small, single to fully double flowers, sometimes in one summer flush, but more often repeating throughout summer. The tiniest are grouped separately as miniature ground-cover roses, but all belong here by virtue of their dense foliage that shades out any weeds that germinate beneath them. Excellent for use over banks or to trail from raised beds.

Miniature bush roses – The smallest of all roses, diminutive in all their parts, miniature bush roses are seldom taller than 45cm (18in) and more often only 25–30cm (10–12in) tall. They are hardy roses of short-jointed, often almost thornless growth, with tiny leaves and clusters of 3–11 small, single to fully double flowers that are borne repeatedly or almost continuously from early summer until the first autumn frosts.

Miniature climbers – Repeat-flowering, hardy and usually very disease-resistant climbers that bear clusters of 3–9 small, single to fully double flowers from summer to autumn. One of the most recent developments in rose-breeding, they are, at present, few in number. They resemble other modern climbers in every way other than in their compact size and habit, seldom exceeding 2.2m (7ft) in height.

Flower shapes

Though a guide only, the classification of flower shapes is as follows:
Flat – single or semi-double flowers that open flat to reveal a central boss of stamens.
Cupped – single or semi-double flowers with incurved petals that form a 'cup' around the central stamens.
Pompon – double or fully double flowers, usually in clusters, that are small, rounded and packed with many tiny petals.

Rounded – double or fully double flowers with petals that overlap to form a bowl-shaped outline.
High-pointed – semi- to fully double flowers with a tight, high-pointed centre, as in many Hybrid Teas.
Urn-shaped – semi- to fully double blooms with incurved inner petals and more spreading outer petals.
Rosette-shaped – an almost flat, semi- to fully double flower packed with short, overlapping petals of uneven size.
Quartered rosette – a rosette-shaped double or fully double flower with petals grouped in four quarters.

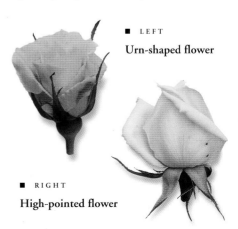

■ LEFT

Urn-shaped flower

■ RIGHT

High-pointed flower

Plant Directory

■ LEFT
'ANGELA RIPPON'
(SYN. 'OCARINA', 'OCARU')

This miniature bush rose has a dense-leaved, upright and bushy habit and is well clothed in glossy dark green, healthy foliage. Throughout summer, it bears clusters of small, rounded, fully double flowers of deep, rich salmon-pink that have a light fragrance. The healthy foliage is a glossy dark green. Good for pots, large window boxes and low edging or hedging. Height 45cm (18in), spread 30cm (12in).

The selection of roses described here are hardy and reliable, and as well as being beautiful, most produce vivacious blooms over many summer months. Most are readily available from garden centres, although a few will require a little searching out from specialist nurseries. Their dimensions are given as guidelines only; sizes always vary slightly according to variable growing conditions.

■ RIGHT
'ANNA FORD'
(SYN. 'HARPICCOLO')

An award-winning Patio rose of compact habit and with a notably good health record. The glossy, dark green leaves provide an admirable foil for the clusters of vibrant orange-red, semi-double, urn-shaped flowers that are produced from summer to autumn. Good for containers, borders and low hedging. Height 45cm (18in), spread 40cm (16in).

■ RIGHT
'APRICOT SUMMER' (SYN. 'KORPAPIRO')

A Patio rose of neat, compact habit that flowers freely
throughout the summer months, bearing a profusion of small,
double, rounded, salmon-apricot blooms in many-flowered
clusters. Useful for pots, window boxes, beds and border edging.
Height 40cm (16in), spread 40cm (16in).

■ ABOVE
'AVON' (SYN. 'POULMULTI')

A low, creeping ground-cover rose of compact habit with
mid-green leaves. The creeping stems are wreathed with clusters
of flat, semi-double, lightly scented blush-pink then pearly-white
flowers from summer to autumn. It is also available as a weeping
standard. Ideal for clothing awkward banks or for a flowering
cascade over a wall. Height 30cm (12in), spread 90cm (36in).

■ BELOW
'BABY LOVE' (SYN. 'SCRIVLUV')

A bushy, upright Patio rose with dense, mid-green foliage
and clusters of cupped, single, short-stemmed, bright
yellow flowers throughout summer. An exceptionally
healthy and floriferous little rose, which, although really
rather tall for most containers, is perfect for beds, borders
and low hedging. Height 1m (39in), spread 75cm (30in).

'CAPTAIN SCARLET'

A stiffly upright miniature climber of compact habit with good disease-resistance; unlike most other larger climbers, it remains clothed to the base with flowers and foliage. The semi-double, rounded, bright red, rather muddled flowers are produced repeatedly from summer to autumn, set off beautifully by dark green foliage that becomes flushed with copper tints in cold weather. Height 2.2m (7ft), spread 1.2m (4ft).

■ ABOVE

'BALLERINA'

A compact Polyantha shrub rose, one of the older small roses, bred in 1937. It has a compact, leafy, upright habit and bears wide clusters of cupped, single, pale pink, white-eyed blooms throughout summer into autumn. A notably floriferous award-winner, but with little scent, it is ideal for borders and low hedging and makes a good specimen for small gardens. Height up to 1.5m (5ft), spread 1m (39in).

■ RIGHT

'BROADLANDS'
(SYN. 'TANMIRSCH')

A vigorous, spreading ground-cover rose forming low mounds of glossy, dark green foliage are wreathed in double, rounded, soft sulphur-yellow, sweetly scented flowers throughout summer into autumn. The colour yellow is unusual among ground-cover roses. It is ideal for clothing awkward banks or for the front of a border. Height 90cm (36in), spread 1.1m (3½ft).

■ ABOVE
'CITY LIGHTS'
(SYN. 'POULGAN')

A vigorous Patio rose with dark
green foliage and wide clusters of
perfectly formed, urn-shaped, fully
double, rich yellow blooms that are
shaded with apricot at their centres.
Flowering throughout summer, it is
perfect for urns, troughs and pots.
Its neat habit also suits border
edging and low hedging. Height
60cm (24in), spread 60cm (24in).

■ RIGHT
'CIDER CUP'
(SYN. 'DICLADIDA')

A Patio rose of compact, bushy
habit with dense, glossy leaves,
producing many-flowered clusters
of small, double, high-pointed
blooms of a lovely warm apricot-
pink throughout summer and
autumn. The neat, upright habit
is well suited to pots, as a standard
and for low hedging. Height 45cm
(18in), spread 30cm (12in).

■ RIGHT
'CONSERVATION'
(SYN. 'COCDIMPLE')

A notably healthy Patio rose of dense, bushy
habit, with small, glossy leaves and a profusion
of cupped, semi-double flowers of warm
apricot-pink borne in well-filled clusters
from summer to autumn. A neat but vigorous
grower, it is perfectly suited to containers
(the colour complements natural stone and
terracotta particularly well) and as low edging.
Height 45cm (18in), spread 45cm (18in).

■ LEFT
'CLIMBING ORANGE
SUNBLAZE'
(SYN. 'CLIMBING
ORANGE MEILLANDINA',
'MEIJIKATARSAR')

An aptly named miniature climber, with
fully double, brilliant, blazing orange-red,
rounded flowers that are produced
from summer to autumn and set off to
perfection against bright green foliage.
It has a well-branched, upright habit
and is perfect for wall training where
space is limited. A climbing sport of
'Orange Sunblaze'. Height 1.5m (5ft),
spread 70cm (28in).

'CRIMSON GEM'

This vigorous miniature
bush is clothed throughout
summer in perfectly
formed, rounded, double,
deep rich red flowers set
off against dark, glossy
foliage. It is a perfect
container rose, especially
good in large window
boxes and containers, and
is equally at home edging
a bed or border. Height
45cm (18in), spread 45cm
(18in).

'FESTIVAL'(SYN. 'KORDIALO')

This Patio rose has a neat, rounded habit
and luxuriant, glossy dark green foliage. The
sumptuously coloured crimson-scarlet double,
rounded blooms open to reveal a centre of gold
and silver, and the pale silvery petal reverse adds
greatly to its charm. Perfect for pots, especially in
pairs set to flank a doorway. Height 60cm (24in),
spread 50cm (20in).

'DARLING FLAME'(SYN. 'MEILUCCA', 'MINUETTO')

A colourful miniature
bush producing clusters
of small, rounded,
double blooms of
vibrant orange-red with
golden anthers. It has
upright growth and
glossy foliage and,
although free-flowering,
is slightly susceptible
to blackspot. Creates
a brilliant ribbon of
colour when used as
edging, and is ideal
for containers.
Height 40cm (16in),
spread 30cm (12in).

■ ABOVE
'FRESH PINK'

This petite Polyantha rose produces large
trusses of rounded, double, clear pink
flowers very freely from summer to
autumn. The graceful habit is displayed
to good effect in large urns or other
containers, and it is equally at home
lending grace and pure colour to a mixed
or shrub border. Height 60–90cm
(24–36in), spread 60–90cm (24–36in).

■ RIGHT
'GLORIA MUNDI'

A compact Polyantha rose with large
clusters of cupped, brilliant orange-red,
semi-double flowers produced almost
continuously throughout the summer
months. It can be used as low hedging
or bedding and in containers and, unlike
many roses, it will tolerate a little shade
and poor soils, although flowering will be
less profuse in these conditions. Height
70cm (28in), spread 70cm (28in).

■ LEFT

'HAKUUN'

A low-growing Patio rose of neat, rounded habit with
exceptionally lovely, creamy white, double, rounded flowers,
buff-tinted in bud and at the petal base, borne in well-filled
clusters from summer to autumn. It has a pleasing light fragrance.
This healthy rose would be perfect in containers sited where the
flowers can be appreciated at close quarters. It is also good for
cut flowers. Height 40cm (16in), spread 45cm (18in).

■ RIGHT

'HAMPSHIRE' (SYN. 'KORHAMP')

One of the 'County' series (named after English counties) of
ground-cover roses, this is a dense and compact bush clothed
from summer to autumn with clusters of stunning, single,
slightly cupped, scarlet blooms with a white eye and a central
boss of golden stamens. The flowers are followed by scarlet hips
in autumn. Equally at home in containers or in open ground in
beds and borders. Height 30cm (12in), spread 60cm (24in).

■ LEFT

'INDIAN SUNBLAZE'
(SYN. 'CAROL-JEAN')

This is a compact miniature bush
with rounded, fully double, deep
pink flowers produced repeatedly
from summer to autumn above
fresh green foliage. Excellent for
containers of all sorts and as low
edging to paths and borders. Height
45cm (18in), spread 45cm (18in).

■ BELOW
'KENT' (SYN. 'WHITE COVER', 'POULCOV', 'PYRENEES')

A compact and spreading ground-cover rose with an excellent health record and good weather resistance. Smothered in large trusses of cupped, short-stemmed, semi-double, pure white flowers from summer to autumn, it is perfect for sunny banks or for the front of mixed and shrub borders. It is also stunning if grown to cascade from tall containers or retaining walls. Height 45cm (18in), spread 1m (3ft).

■ LEFT
'LAURA FORD' (SYN. 'CHEWARVEL')

For the walls of a small courtyard or patio, this miniature climber's stiffly upright growth is ideal. The small, scented, semi-double, urn-shaped flowers, borne continuously from summer to autumn, are yellow, developing a hint of pink as they age, opening almost flat to reveal a boss of golden stamens. Height 2.2m (7ft), spread 1.2m (4ft).

'LITTLE WHITE PET'
(SYN. 'WHITE PET')

A vigorous but diminutive Polyantha rose of light, airy habit, with clusters of beautifully formed, rosette-shaped flowers borne throughout summer. Pink in bud, they are white when fully open and have a light scent; the flower form is almost identical to 'Félicité Perpétue', the well-known rambler of which it is a sport. Ideal for the front of a border and very elegant in containers, it is also exquisite for miniature flower arrangements. Height 45cm (18in), spread 55cm (22in).

'LADY PENELOPE'

A stiffly upright miniature climber of neat habit, with mid-green leaves and rounded, fully double, salmon-pink flowers borne repeatedly from summer to autumn. A healthy rose that remains clothed to the base with flowers and foliage, it is ideal for walls in confined spaces and for smaller gardens. Height 2.2m (7ft), spread 1.2m (4ft).

'MINI METRO'
(SYN. 'FINSTAR', 'RUFIN')

A miniature bush with fresh green foliage and clusters of well-formed, rounded, fully double, apricot-orange flowers that open to reveal golden stamens. Flowering throughout summer, it is ideal for pots, window boxes and other containers. Height 40cm (16in), spread 25cm (10in).

■ ABOVE
'MR BLUEBIRD'

A miniature rose of bushy, compact habit bearing airy sprays of many small, cupped, semi-double, white-eyed flowers in shades of reddish purple, from summer to autumn. With such a novel and unusual colour, this healthy little rose is perfect for window boxes, pots and other containers, or as an edging to beds and borders. Height 30cm (12in), spread 25cm (10in).

■ RIGHT
'NICE DAY'
(SYN. 'CHEWSEA',
'PATIO QUEEN')

Clusters of small, double, urn-shaped flowers of warm peachy pink with a light sweet scent are borne from summer to autumn on this petite climber. It is excellent for a low wall or trellis where space is confined; the perfectly formed buds are ideal as buttonholes and for flower arrangements. Height 2.2m (7ft), spread 1m (3ft).

■ LEFT
'NORTHAMPTONSHIRE' (SYN. 'MATTDOR')

A vigorous, low-growing ground-cover rose with dense, glossy dark green foliage and dainty sprays of perfectly formed, cupped, soft pink flowers from summer to autumn. This spreading rose has an excellent health record and is good for clothing sunny banks, for trailing over retaining walls, or for the front of a mixed border; the petite flowers make ideal boutonnières. Height 45cm (18in), spread 1m (3ft).

■ RIGHT
'ORANGES AND LEMONS' (SYN. 'MACORANLEM')

A compact cluster-flowered bush with shiny dark green leaves that are flushed copper when young. It bears heavy clusters of rounded, double flowers from summer to autumn, striped and partly coloured scarlet-orange on a creamy golden yellow ground. Perhaps too large for all but the most substantial of containers, this sunny little rose is ideal for low hedging, and massed plantings in beds and borders. Height 80cm (32in), spread 60cm (24in).

■ LEFT
'ORANGE SUNBLAZE' (SYN. 'MEIJIKATAR', 'ORANGE MEILLANDINA')

A bushy miniature rose with ample bright green foliage and profuse clusters of small, cupped, semi-double flowers of brilliant, vivid orange-red with golden centres, produced from summer to autumn. Excellent for containers of all sorts, and as low edging to paths and borders. Height 30cm (12in), spread 30cm (12in).

■ BELOW

'OXFORDSHIRE' (SYN. 'KORFULLWIND')

An award-winning, spreading ground-cover rose with cascading stems wreathed in double clear pink rounded flowers almost continuously from summer to autumn. Ideal for sunny banks, it also looks stunning when grown as a standard or in hanging baskets. Height 60cm (2ft), spread 1.5m (5ft).

■ RIGHT

'PERLE D'OR'
(SYN. 'YELLOW
CÉCILE BRÜNNER')

One of the older small roses, this petite Polyantha bush has a dense habit of growth, ample dark green foliage, and dainty sprays of scented, diminutive but exquisitely formed, urn-shaped flowers of creamy honey-yellow flushed with pink, lasting from summer to autumn. Almost thornless, it is ideal for a mixed border or for large urns and containers. Height 1.2m (4ft), spread 1m (3ft).

■ ABOVE

'PEEK A BOO'
(SYN. 'BRASS RING',
'DICGROW')

A neat, cushion-forming Patio rose with a slightly spreading habit and well-filled clusters of small but beautifully formed, rounded, double flowers of a gentle, rich peachy apricot that gradually fade to pink as they mature. It is perfect for containers and urns, and for cutting to use in flower arrangements. Height 45cm (18in), spread 45cm (18in).

■ BELOW
'PRETTY POLLY'
(SYN. 'MEITONJE', 'SWEET
SUNBLAZE', 'PINK SYMPHONY')

A dense, rounded and well-named Patio
rose with plentiful glossy dark green
foliage. Blooming from summer to autumn,
the beautifully formed, rounded, fully
double flowers, borne in well-filled clusters,
have a light sweet scent and are of a
particularly pretty clear pink. It looks well
in terracotta containers and window boxes,
and would make a beautiful ribbon of
colour if grown as low edging. Height
40cm (16in), spread 45cm (18in).

■ LEFT
'QUEEN MOTHER'
(SYN. 'KORQUEMU')

A delightful little Patio rose with
plentiful dark glossy foliage and
clusters of cupped, semi-double
flowers with slightly wavy petals
of a delicate, soft clear pink, borne
in profusion throughout summer
into autumn. Ideal for containers,
including hanging baskets and
large window boxes. Height 40cm
(16in), spread 60cm (24in).

■ LEFT
'RED ACE'
(SYN. 'AMANDA',
'AMRUDA')

One of the most sumptuous reds
among the miniature roses, this little
bush has a neat, leafy habit and
produces clusters of rounded, semi-
double, rich crimson blooms from
summer to autumn. They are perfect
for cutting, and this variety makes
fine edging to a border, dramatic
massed plantings and a beautiful
specimen for containers. Height
30cm (12in), spread 30cm (12in).

■ RIGHT
'RED MEIDILAND'
(SYN. 'MEINEBLE',
'ROUGE
MEILLANDÉCAR')

A dense, compact ground-cover
rose with clusters of relatively
large, deep red, single, cupped
flowers with white centres and
a boss of golden stamens, borne
almost continuously from
summer to autumn and
followed by small red hips.
It is suitable for the front of a
shrub or mixed border, and is
particularly useful for clothing
sunny banks or trailing over a
retaining wall. Height 75cm
(30in), spread 1.5m (5ft).

■ LEFT
'RISE 'N' SHINE' (SYN. 'GOLDEN MEILLANDINA', 'GOLDEN SUNBLAZE')

A miniature bush rose of neat, compact habit producing clusters of small but well-formed, fully double, urn-shaped, sunny yellow flowers with pointed petals, from summer right through to autumn. Use in containers of all sorts, and as low edging in formal beds and borders. Height 40cm (16in), spread 25cm (10in).

■ RIGHT
'SCARLET MEIDILAND' (SYN. 'MEIKROTAL')

A ground-cover shrub rose with ample, glossy foliage and large, heavy clusters of many small, cherry-red, rounded, double blooms with golden stamens, produced in abundance from summer onwards; the autumn flushes of flower are notably profuse. It is suitable for the middle ranks of a shrub or mixed border, and for low hedging and containers; it even tolerates light shade. Height 90cm (3ft), spread 1.8m (6ft).

■ LEFT
'SUN HIT' (SYN. 'POULSUN')

A compact Patio rose of upright habit bearing sunny golden-yellow, fully double, urn-shaped blooms with moderately good scent in great profusion from summer to autumn. Bred as a pot-rose, its small stature is ideally suited to containers and window boxes, and it can also be brought into the house when in bloom. Also available as a standard. Height 45cm (18in), spread 45cm (18in).

■ BELOW
'SUSSEX' (SYN. 'POULAV')

A vigorous ground-cover rose producing masses of flowers from early summer to autumn; the fully double, rounded, neatly formed flowers are a soft apricot-pink. Ideal on a sunny bank, at the front of a border and in large planters. Height 45cm (18in), spread 90cm (36in).

■ ABOVE
'SURREY' (SYN. 'KORLANUM', 'SOMMERWIND', 'VENT D'ÉTÉ')

A robust ground-cover rose that looks superb in large containers, in borders or as a specimen. It has a leafy habit, producing dense mounds of foliage and long stems wreathed with abundant clusters of double, cupped, warm-pink flowers from summer to autumn. Height 90cm (3ft), spread 1.2m (4ft).

■ RIGHT
'SWANY' (SYN. 'MEIBURENAC')

A bushy, spreading and very elegant ground-cover rose with plentiful dark green, slightly bronzed, very glossy foliage that acts as a perfect foil to the wreathing clusters of flat, double, pure white flowers. It is suitable for containers – especially charming in a formal courtyard setting – and in mixed borders. Height 90cm (3ft), spread 1.5m (5ft).

■ ABOVE
'SWEET MAGIC'
(SYN. 'DICMAGIC')

An attractive, award-winning Patio rose with
dense, bright green foliage and full clusters of
scented, double, rounded soft apricot-orange
and yellow flowers that are borne freely from
summer to autumn. A perfect container
specimen and ideal for edging. Height 40cm
(16in), spread 40cm (16in).

■ RIGHT
'SWEET DREAM'
(SYN. 'FRYMINICOT')

A neat, upright Patio rose with moderate
scent and a very attractive 'old-fashioned'
flower form; a deserving award-winner.
The fully double, lightly scented warm
apricot-pink flowers are in quartered-rosette
form and borne in abundant clusters from
summer to autumn. Elegant in containers
or as ribbon edging to paths and beds.
Height 40cm (16in), spread 35cm (14in).

■ RIGHT
'THE FAIRY'

A sweet Polyantha rose, a deserving award-winner with a good health record, that blooms almost continuously from late summer to autumn. It has a dense, spreading, cushion-like habit, and bears dainty sprays of small, fully double, very pretty rosette-shaped flowers in pale pink. Lovely in a shrub or mixed border and elegant in containers. Height 60cm (2ft), spread 1.2m (4ft).

■ LEFT
'TOP MARKS'
(SYN. 'FRYMINISTAR')

A neat, cushion-forming Patio rose with abundant glossy foliage and well-filled clusters of double, rounded, brilliant orange-vermilion flowers from summer to autumn. An award-winning rose, it is suitable for edging borders and bedding, and makes a striking specimen in containers. Height 40cm (16in), spread 45cm (18in).

■ RIGHT
'WARM WELCOME' (SYN. 'CHEWIZZ')

A glossy-leaved miniature climber producing small, semi-double, urn-shaped, bright orange-vermilion flowers freely and almost continuously from summer to autumn. Good for walls in small courtyards or where space is restricted. Height 2.2m (7ft), spread 2.2m (7ft).

■ ABOVE

'WHITE CÉCILE
BRÜNNER'

A diminutive Polyantha
bush bred at the turn of
the century, with plentiful
dark green foliage and dainty
sprays of sweet-scented,
beautifully fully double,
urn-shaped white flowers,
faintly peach-tinted, borne
almost continuously from
summer to autumn. Almost
thornless, it is ideal for a
mixed border or for large
urns and other substantial
containers. A perfect
buttonhole flower. Height
1m (3ft), spread 1m (3ft).

■ ABOVE

'WHITE FLOWER CARPET'
(SYN. 'SCHNEEFLOCKE')

A dense, dark-leaved, almost evergreen
ground-cover shrub with an excellent
health record. Mounds of foliage offset
clusters of large, cupped, semi-double
white flowers, borne from summer to
autumn. Excellent on a sunny bank,
as a standard or trailing over a wall.
There are red and pink forms too.
Height 75cm (30in), spread 1.2m (4ft).

■ LEFT

'WILTSHIRE'
(SYN. 'KORMUSE')

A spreading ground-cover shrub that
is excellent for banks and planters. The
dense glossy foliage is almost obscured by
large clusters of lightly scented, rounded,
double, deep reddish-pink flowers borne
from summer to autumn. Height 60cm
(2ft), spread 1.2m (4ft).

The Grower's Guide

Buying miniature roses

Choosing new roses for the garden is one of the most enjoyable of all gardening activities, for it carries with it the anticipation of many years of pleasure from these generally long-lived shrubs. It is most important to consider the space that you have available and to select a rose variety of a suitable size so that it will not rapidly outgrow the allotted space. Proportion becomes all the more important if you wish to grow roses in containers.

There are several ways to make your selection, all of them pleasurable. You can look through gardening books and specialist rose catalogues at leisure by the fireside

while you plan your plantings for the following season, or you can visit garden centres to make your selection. But perhaps the most enjoyable way of selecting roses is to visit gardens in your locality, where they can be observed in growth and flower, so that you can take note of any that attract your attention. Many of the specialist nurseries have rose gardens attached to the nursery, and most encourage buyers to visit their rose fields during the summer.

Ideally, you should make several visits (and this is no great hardship, after all) so that you can check on their continuity of flowering performance and their overall health and vigour. In any rose collection you will notice individual cultivars that are markedly more free-flowering or healthy and disease-resistant. If any of these roses suit your purpose, you would be well advised to grow them in preference to those that perform less well – good disease-resistance does much to reduce the necessity of repeated applications of chemical pesticides and fungicides.

Once you have decided on a rose that appeals to you and that suits the location and the purpose for which it is to be used, you have to set about finding it. Many garden centres carry

■ BELOW
The roots of container-grown roses should fill the pot but should not be so crowded as to spiral around upon themselves.

R. 'Cécile Brünner' is a perennial
favourite; healthy and floriferous,
it is perfect in this elegant container.

a wide range of container-grown roses
and, with luck, the one you want will
be in stock. Buying in this way has
the advantage that you can check over
the plant yourself before purchase.

Look for a plant that is free from
obvious signs of pests such as aphids,
which generally cluster at the soft
shoot tips, and diseases such as rust or
blackspot, which infect the foliage.
Top growth should have a well-
balanced framework of sturdy shoots,
well clothed in ample healthy foliage
of good colour – avoid purchasing
any with sparse or yellowed foliage,
or with evidence of leaf drop, which
may indicate that the plant has been
starved of nutrients or moisture. Such
plants seldom establish well. The
container should be well filled with
healthy roots, and the growing
medium should be evenly moist –
neither dry not waterlogged – and
clean of surface weeds. While the

preferred planting season is between
late autumn and early spring, garden
centres may have roses in stock
throughout much of the growing
season. If you buy during the summer
months, they will almost certainly be
in flower, and should be rigorously
deadheaded before planting.

If you cannot find the rose you
want at a garden centre, you need
to look to a specialist supplier,
preferably one that is a member
of your national Rose Growers'
Association. Most national rose
societies produce 'who grows what'
booklets, which list roses and the
nurseries that supply them. Many
national horticultural societies also

sponsor publications of general plant
lists and supplying nurseries. These
leaflets are absolutely indispensable
when tracing the less well-known
cultivars. You can buy happily from
a reputable nursery, either directly
or by mail order, for they strive
constantly to produce good, healthy
stock and will guarantee that their
plants are well grown and true to
name. Most will also replace without
quibble any that are unsatisfactory
when your order arrives.

Many specialist nurseries have extensive
rose gardens to display their wares and
to help you make your choice.

Planting and growing miniature roses

Roses are not difficult plants to grow well, provided that their basic needs for light, moisture, nutrients and good air circulation are met. Many of the modern miniatures and other small roses are easier than most since, in general, they have been bred with hardiness, disease-resistance and good productivity in mind.

There is one extremely important consideration, however, when planting roses of any type: they should not be planted in soil where other roses have grown before, because of the risk of a syndrome known as 'rose soil sickness' or 'rose replant disease'. Rose sickness is not clearly understood, but it appears to result from a combination of nutrient depletion and a build-up of

micro-organisms – fungi, nematodes (eelworms) and viruses – around the roots of the old plant. These micro-organisms become particularly virulent when in contact with the newly formed feeder roots of a freshly planted young rose. There is no cure, so the problem should be avoided in the first place. If you really do need to replace a rose with another in the same site, you must remove the soil, taking out a 'cube' of about 50 x 50cm (20 x 20in) by at least 50cm (20in) deep and replace it with fresh soil that has not had roses grown in it previously.

Roses prefer a position in full sun but will tolerate light dappled shade, and, especially when grown in containers or in climates with long,

hot summers, will positively appreciate a little shade from the hottest midday sun. As with most plants, they dislike being placed directly under trees, or too close to any other plants that will compete at the root zone for nutrients and moisture. Similarly, they prefer an open site but with some shelter from strong winds.

It is particularly important to bear this in mind when siting roses in containers around the house. Where wind is channelled between buildings or other impermeable structures, the 'wind funnel' effect builds up speed to searing proportions, and virtually no plant will thrive in such severe conditions. High-speed wind causes the plant to lose moisture more quickly than it is able to replace it, and so it suffers drought effects; the plant will not thrive, and in severe circumstances may even die. The effect of strong wind is even less tolerable when plants are in pots and containers, because they have a very limited soil volume from which to draw moisture.

While the ideal soil is the almost mythical fertile, moisture-retentive but well-drained loam, they will thrive in most soils provided they are not too dry or boggy and

■ RIGHT
Group small roses in containers of different sizes and shapes create an attractive feature near the front door, in a courtyard or to decorate a patio.

■ LEFT
The soft pink of *R*. 'Queen Mother'
is a perfect complement to the soft
grey of this stoneware container.

waterlogged. And all soils, whether
light and sandy or heavy clay, can be
improved before planting to make
them more suitable. Indeed, roses are
capable of giving you many years of
pleasure, and deserve – and will
reward amply – effort spent in
thorough soil preparation.

Feeding and weeding

As a group, roses have a reputation
for being greedy feeders; the
production of flowers over many
months demands considerable
energy, and even roses that are
capable of continuous flowering will
fail to do so if not fed sufficiently.
They need an application of fertilizer
on planting and regularly thereafter.
The incorporation of organic matter
provides a degree of nutrition, but
its main advantage is to enhance
drainage and moisture retention
while increasing the soil's ability
to hold nutrients within it.

In the season before planting,
clear the site thoroughly of all weeds,
paying special attention to deep-
rooting perennial weeds, such as
couch grass and dandelions. Weeds
not only compete for light, moisture
and nutrients; they also often act as
alternative hosts to a range of pests

■ RIGHT
When large climbing
or rambling roses
are trained to form a
flowery 'ceiling' at the
top of a pergola, they
often become bare at
the base, so combine
them with miniature
climbers to clothe the
pillars or uprights.

and diseases. Weed clearance must
be especially thorough if you are
planting ground-cover roses; you
will find it a painful and tedious
experience to have to hand-weed
among their thorny stems later on.

On small areas, weeding can
easily be done by forking over and
removing weeds by hand. On larger
areas, you may wish to use a systemic
herbicide based on glyphosate, which
is transferred through the whole plant,
killing the roots as well as top growth.

If you garden organically, cover
the area with old carpet, black plastic
or other light-excluding material for
a growing season prior to planting.
Alternatively, if you have patience,
you can use a flame weeder, a hand-
held flame gun that is passed slowly
over the weed so that the heat
destroys the internal cell structures.
This is excellent for small annual
weeds, but you have to treat
repeatedly to clear the site completely
of deep-rooted perennial weeds.

Planting in open ground

Once the site has been thoroughly cleared of weeds, dig over the planting site, and incorporate plenty of organic matter in the form of garden compost or well-rotted manure. It is best to do this at least three to four weeks before planting.

Before planting, water the plant in its container and set aside to drain; if the compost (soil mix) is very dry, soak in a bucket of water until thoroughly wetted. Make the planting hole large enough to hold the roots without restriction and, before planting, gently tease out the roots from the compost so that they do not grow in spiral fashion around the hole. Backfilling is best done in several stages, firming with gentle heel pressure between each to remove air pockets and ensure that all roots make intimate contact with the soil.

Many small and ground-cover roses are grown on their own roots, but if the plant is grafted, be sure to set the graft union 2.5cm (1in) below soil level. Most are container-grown, but if you obtain plants bare-rooted in the dormant season, keep the roots moist until planting. If the soil is too wet or frozen, bare-root plants can be heeled in – planted in a trench with the roots covered with loose soil – until growing conditions improve.

PLANTING CONTAINERIZED ROSES

1 Make a planting hole the same depth as and twice the width of the container, to allow the roots sufficient room to grow unrestricted.

2 Loosen the soil at the bottom of the hole using a hand fork, and incorporate a dressing of slow-release fertilizer into the bottom of the hole.

5 Backfill with soil in two or three stages, firming thoroughly as you go by applying gentle pressure with the heel of your foot.

6 Apply a top-dressing of slow-release fertilizer around the root zone, at the manufacturer's recommended rate, and fork it in.

3 Place the plant in its pot into the hole and use a cane to check the depth. The cane should skim the top of the compost (soil mix) surface in the pot.

4 Slide the plant gently from its pot and tease out the roots carefully. Place the plant in the hole and spread the roots evenly around the hole.

7 Water in thoroughly and plentifully using a watering can with a fine rose, to avoid soil capping or washing any top soil away.

8 Apply a layer of organic mulch 5–8cm (2–3in) deep to the area around the root zone to conserve soil moisture and suppress weed growth.

SPACING AND COLOUR ASSOCIATIONS

When planting in open ground, check the estimated spread of each plant and set them this distance apart. If planting for formal effects, choose plants of similar dimensions to ensure uniformity. For an informal effect, choose roses of a graceful habit, such as the Polyanthas.

While colour associations are largely a matter of taste, hot tones of orange-vermilion can be difficult to place and may tend to dominate. They do, however, associate well with dark-leaved shrubs like *Cotinus coggygria* 'Royal Purple', *Acer palmatum* f. *atropurpureum*, *Cercis canadensis* 'Forest Pansy' or *Corylus maxima* 'Purpurea'.

Magenta combines perfectly with grey-leaved plants – stachys and artemisias – and especially with the grey-purple tones of *Salvia officinalis* 'Purpurascens'. Soft apricots, yellows and clear pinks are all complementary to shades of blue, such as lavenders, campanulas, delphiniums and the intense blues of *Salvia guaranitica* or violet-blues of *S. × sylvestris* cultivars.

Planting in containers

Choose a container that suits the final size and habit of growth of your chosen rose. A tall container is best for the gracefully arching types and trailing ground-cover roses; a shorter, wider container suits more bushy roses. Decide on the final placement of your container and plant it up *in situ*; it will be very heavy and difficult to move once planted. It is best to site your containers where a water source is readily accessible; they will need watering daily in periods of warm, dry weather.

There are several types of growing medium or compost (soil mix) available, based on loam, peat or peat substitutes like coir or bark. Peat-based composts are lightweight but do not hold nutrients well, and you usually need to apply extra fertilizer after about six weeks. They are also extremely difficult to re-wet if allowed to dry out. Loam-based potting mixes are more suitable for permanent plantings, as they retain nutrients for longer, so that they are available to the roots. They also

lend greater weight and stability and, should you forget to water, are more easily re-wetted than peat-based composts.

To guarantee free drainage from the bottom of the pot, use 'pot feet' to keep the pot clear of the ground. Free drainage is especially important if you intend to leave the pots outdoors over winter; it helps prevent soil water from freezing and cracking the pot. In frost-prone climates, protect the roots by wrapping pots in horticultural fleece or similar.

GROWING ROSES IN CONTAINERS

1 Cover the drainage holes at the bottom of the pot with a layer of broken pots, to keep the compost (soil mix) from dropping through and to improve drainage.

2 Add a 5–8cm (2–3in) layer of grit or gravel for drainage and stability, then fill the pot with planting medium, allowing a 2.5cm (1in) space below the pot rim to permit thorough watering.

3 Make a planting hole large enough to hold the root ball (roots) without restriction and check the depth. Slide the plant gently from its pot and loosen the roots, then place it in the hole.

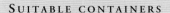

SUITABLE CONTAINERS

Provided that a container is large enough to hold the root ball (roots) and has holes in the bottom for drainage, you can use all sorts of containers – new or reclaimed – for roses. Plastic pots are lightweight and dry out less rapidly than stone or terracotta ones, but pots made of natural materials often have the edge aesthetically, and their greater weight lends stability.

■ LEFT
The finished article; the hot colours of this Patio rose, *R.* 'Top Marks', are enhanced by the warm tints of this glazed stoneware pot, while its shape and size are in perfect balance with the size and habit of the rose.

4 Carefully backfill with the growing medium in stages, firming the compost gently with your fingers between each stage to ensure good contact between the roots and growing medium.

5 Apply a top-dressing of slow-release fertilizer following the manufacturer's recommended rate, or insert a pellet of proprietary slow-release fertilizer below the surface.

6 Water in thoroughly, until excess water drains from the bottom of the pot. If desired, add a further top-dressing of grit for decoration and to help retain moisture and suppress weeds.

Planting in a hanging basket

Choose a hanging basket to suit the size of the rose; a 35–40cm (14–16in) basket will hold three or four ground-cover roses, but you can use smaller baskets for single plantings.

To conserve water, line the basket with sphagnum moss and then insert a plastic liner with drainage holes pierced in it. As long as you remember to feed the established plants regularly, the lighter weight of peat-based growing mixes and composts is more easily managed in a hanging basket.

Hang the planted basket in place before watering thoroughly; a large basket will be too heavy to lift safely when it has been well watered. If you want to create a mixed planting with annuals or small trailing perennials, plant these around the base of the rose before watering.

Once planted, the basket may be stored in a sheltered place outdoors or, if planted in late winter, in a cold greenhouse until spring, to allow the plants to become well established before being exposed to the elements.

Because hanging baskets are more exposed to wind, they dry out more rapidly than other containers. They are likely to need watering every day in warm weather, so place them where water is easily accessible.

■ ABOVE
As a rose in a hanging basket grows, it will disguise most of the basket and moss.

Most garden centres stock pump-action, high-level watering devices that will make the task easier.

GROWING ROSES IN HANGING BASKETS

1 Line the hanging basket with a layer of sphagnum moss, which looks attractive and can also hold many times its own weight of water.

2 To conserve even more moisture, add a second lining of black plastic into which a number of holes have been pierced to permit free drainage.

3 Add a layer of the potting medium of your choice, insert the plant and backfill firmly with more soil mix. Hang the basket and water it thoroughly.

Pegging down ground-cover roses

Ground-cover roses are planted in the same way as other roses. As they grow, the stems of trailing sorts often root where they touch the ground – a form of natural layering – creating extensive mounds of foliage and flowers. You can help this process along by pegging down the stems into the soil with a wooden peg or U-shaped piece of wire. Place the stem where you wish it to root, and just beneath a node (leaf joint), cultivate the soil with a hand fork and make a shallow depression, 5–8cm (2–3in) deep. Peg the stem down into the depression, and bend the growing tip upwards so that it emerges from the far side of the depression. Cover the pegged section with soil and firm gently. Keep it moist until it is well rotted and able to seek its own moisture supply from the surrounding soil.

You can improve the effectiveness of ground cover with these roses by planting through a sheet mulch of permeable woven landscaping fabric. This material suppresses weeds, conserves moisture and, by reducing rain splash, keeps foliage and flowers clean and pristine. It also keeps the roots cool in summer and helps prevent freezing in winter. The fabric is laid down over weed-free soil, and a

PEGGING DOWN

1 Bend down the selected shoot to soil level. When it meets the soil, cultivate with a fork and make a shallow depression, 5–8cm (2–3in) deep.

2 Peg the shoot into the depression with a bent piece of wire at a leaf joint, leaving the stem tip to emerge free from the far side of the depression. Cover the pegged section with soil, and firm in.

planting hole is cut into it by making two slits at right angles to each other. Dig a planting hole through the gap and plant the rose as usual, watering in thoroughly. Then fold back the fabric over the root zone. Landscaping fabric is not attractive, but you can top-dress it with gravel or an ornamental mulch such as cocoa shells or bark. Since the fabric is permeable, you can feed by top-dressing around the roots with fertilizer, which will be washed down to the roots by natural rainfall.

Care and maintenance

Small roses need very little in the way of annual maintenance, but there are several routine tasks that will ensure that your roses give of their best, and continue to do so, to provide many years of pleasure.

Mulching

One of the most important requirements is to maintain a 5–8cm (2–3in) mulch of well-rotted organic matter in the form of farmyard manure or garden compost at the root zone. An organic mulch helps to keep the soil in good health, and improves aeration and drainage. It also makes it better able to retain moisture and nutrients that the plants can use. A mulch prevents soil 'capping' during heavy rain; the weight of raindrops – especially on heavy clay or silty soils – can cause compaction at the soil surface, preventing free movement of air and water to the root zone, to the detriment of root function. Mulch also helps to reduce temperature fluctuations at the root zone, keeping roots cool in summer and preventing them from freezing in winter. Finally, a mulch helps to reduce weeds, which compete for light, moisture and nutrients. Mulches should be applied

each or every other year around the base of the plant, in early spring, in periods of fine weather. The soil should be moist but not waterlogged or frozen. If you apply a mulch to dry soil, it reduces the amount of natural rainfall that can reach the roots.

Weeding

It is essential to keep your roses weed-free, especially during the growing season. However, repeated hoeing is not the best way to do this, since it is likely to damage the fine feeder roots that are close to the soil's surface. If you have a large area to look after, hoe if necessary, but avoid an area about 0.6–1m (2–3ft) across around the base of each plant. This can then be weeded by hand; weeds are easily pulled from the loose surface mulch.

Watering

Roses need adequate moisture throughout the growing season. Plants in open ground, especially if well mulched, seldom need additional water except during the establishment period, or when hot, dry weather is prolonged. In this case, the soil may be dry to some depth, so applications of water must be copious enough to penetrate the soil around the root zone. Watering too little causes the plant's roots to grow up towards the surface in search of moisture, thus becoming vulnerable to the damaging effects of heat and drought.

Plants in containers rely heavily on the gardener to be conscientious in watering. They have only a small volume of soil to exploit for moisture, and the soil in pots dries rapidly in warm, dry weather. This is especially true of roses grown in hanging baskets. Terracotta pots, which are permeable to water, need more attention than plastic ones. During the summer, all container-grown roses should be checked and watered thoroughly – every day, if necessary.

■ LEFT
Remove weeds from the root zone by hand to avoid damaging fine feeder roots.

Feeding

Roses have high nutrient requirements, especially those that expend much energy in producing flowers repeatedly throughout the summer. To keep them growing and flowering well, apply a balanced general fertilizer or a specific rose fertilizer, which is higher in potash, in early spring just after pruning and before growth really gets underway. Repeat just as the first flush of flowers begins. If they are not growing and flowering well, give another application of a high potash fertilizer in late summer or early autumn; this also helps late-formed shoots ripen

Apply fertilizer to the base of the plant and 'tickle' it in with a hand fork.

before the onset of winter. Soil nutrients in containers tend to leach away more quickly than in open ground so, in addition to routine applications of fertilizer, give extra fertilizer every two or three weeks in the form of a liquid feed applied when you water, or as a foliar spray.

Pests and diseases

As soon as the weather begins to warm up in spring, be vigilant for the first signs of pest and disease infestation, and treat immediately, before population numbers have time to build up. Aphids are particularly damaging, as they attack young shoot tips and cause subsequent distortion of growth. If you look after the soil, roses generally grow well and remain healthy, but in some seasons, poor weather provides perfect conditions for the spread of fungal diseases, especially blackspot. An annual tar-oil winter wash of stems and surrounding soil, along with the collection and burning of fallen leaves, will reduce the reservoir of fungal spores and the need for extensive spraying with fungicide later on. A spray with a specific rose fungicide, when the first leaves have emerged fully, can be applied as a preventative

Cut back faded flowers to a bud in the axil of the nearest full-sized leaf.

measure. Many modern roses have some resistance to blackspot, but if you see it developing, another spray in early summer and again in mid-summer helps keep it in check.

Deadheading

It is particularly important for roses that flower repeatedly to be deadheaded. If they are allowed to produce hips, the energy expended in seed production is unavailable for further production of flowers.

For cluster-flowered roses, removing the central flower of the cluster as it fades will improve the appearance of the group. When the entire cluster has faded, remove the whole head, cutting back with an angled cut to a healthy bud or full-sized leaf. For those that produce a solitary flower, cut back to a healthy outward-facing bud or full-sized leaf.

Propagation

As with all plants that are complex hybrids, propagation by seed is not recommended for roses other than true species, because even if seed is produced, it will not come true to type. Most roses are produced by bud-grafting, whereby buds of the desired cultivar are grafted on to a rootstock of another vigorous-rooted rose. This is a highly skilled technique that is generally unsuitable for the amateur, not least because rootstocks have to be pre-prepared and are not easily available.

Taking semi-ripe or hardwood cuttings, and by layering are simple techniques that are more likely to be successful for the amateur gardener. But, with the possible exception of the ground-cover roses – many of which are increased commercially by cuttings – it is important to bear in mind that roses of complex breeding may not be as vigorous as their grafted counterparts when increased by cuttings or layers.

Semi-ripe cuttings

It is best to take semi-ripe cuttings from mid- to late summer from the current season's growth, when the base of new shoots is just beginning to ripen, that is, to turn hard and woody. In regions with very cold winters, semi-ripe cuttings may prove more successful than hardwood ones, although they need more attention in providing suitable conditions for rooting, and need extra care during their first winter as younger plants.

Take a healthy shoot or sideshoot and remove it from the parent plant, cutting just above an outward-facing bud. Trim the cutting at the base, just below a leaf joint, and remove the soft tip just above a leaf or bud, to leave a cutting about 10cm (4in)

TAKING SEMI-RIPE CUTTINGS

1 Using clean, sharp secateurs (pruners), remove a shoot or sideshoot from the parent plant, cutting it just above an outward-facing bud. Pinch out the soft growing tip just above a leaf or bud.

2 Trim the base of each cutting just below a leaf joint to make a cutting about 10cm (4in) long. You may get more than one cutting from each shoot.

3 Remove the lower leaves and all of the thorns, then, using a sharp blade, wound the base of the stem by removing the thinnest sliver of bark, about 1cm (½in) long, from one side of the stem.

long. Carefully remove the lower leaves and all thorns. Wound the base by shaving off a sliver of bark, about 1cm (½in) long, from one side of the stem, using a very sharp knife or scalpel. Do not cut too deeply; you are aiming just to remove the outer bark. Dip the base of the cutting in a hormone rooting compound.

Prepare a half pot by filling it with a mix of equal parts of peat and perlite, or peat and sharp sand. Water it thoroughly and allow to drain. Using a dibber to make a hole in the compost (soil mix), insert the cutting to two-thirds of its length,

and firm in gently with the fingers to ensure contact between the stem and the compost. You can fit three to six cuttings in a 12cm (5in) pot, but make sure that the leaves of the cuttings do not touch each other. Mist over with a fungicide spray, to thoroughly moisten the cutting and compost surface. Do not forget to label with the plant name and date, and then place the pot in a closed propagating case with bottom heat at 18–21°C (64–70°F). Keep the cuttings in good light but avoid direct sunlight, which causes overheating and will rapidly 'cook' the cuttings.

Check the plants regularly, and remove fallen leaves as soon as you see them; if left in place, they will rot and spread fungal infection to the cuttings. Keep the cuttings evenly moist by watering or misting with a fungicide solution. Roots will begin to form within six to eight weeks, and by late autumn or early winter you can gradually admit more air to the propagator to wean them from their protected environment. A frost-free greenhouse is ideal protection during the winter months. By the following spring, they should be sufficiently well rooted to pot them separately.

4 Dip the base of the cutting in a hormone rooting compound and tap off any excess powder. If using a liquid preparation, decant a small amount to avoid any contamination of the remainder.

5 Insert the prepared cutting into a half pot of moistened cutting compost. Dibble a hole with a dibber, and push in the cutting one-third of its length. Firm in with the fingers.

6 Insert 3–6 cuttings in the same pot, making sure that their leaves do not touch. Mist with fungicide and place the pot in a closed, heated propagator in bright, indirect light.

Grow the cuttings on in pots for their first summer in a sheltered place outdoors or in an open cold frame, and they will be ready to plant out in the autumn.

Hardwood cuttings

Use the fully ripened stems of the current season's growth for hardwood cuttings; this is best done in early autumn. They are easier to manage than semi-ripe cuttings, and need no special equipment and minimal aftercare. Hardwood cuttings are an ideal method for true miniatures and the Patio, Polyantha and ground-cover roses, whether trailing or bushy.

Prepare a trench in a sheltered part of the garden, about 20–25cm (8–10in) deep, and fill it to about one-third of its depth with sharp sand. Take a strong, well-ripened stem from the parent plant, remove the soft tip and cut it into 23cm (9in) lengths, with the basal cut just below a leaf joint. Remove all of the lower leaves, but leave two at the top of each cutting.

Dip the stem base in hormone rooting compound and insert the cuttings in the trench to the depth of the uppermost two leaves. Firm them in carefully, water in thoroughly and

label with the plant name and date. Check them after frosty weather, as freezing may cause the soil to 'heave' and disturb the cuttings; if this happens, re-firm carefully. They can be given an occasional liquid feed during the summer. The cuttings should be well rooted by the following autumn, when they can be lifted and transferred to their flowering site if they are sufficiently well developed; if not, leave them in place and transplant them in the following spring.

A variation on this technique is sometimes used for miniature and

ground-cover roses that may not produce stems of sufficient length for the technique described.

Cuttings are trimmed to about 8cm (3in) long, and are rooted in small pots in a cold greenhouse with gentle bottom heat at 21°C (70°F). They root and grow on much more quickly, and can usually be planted out the following spring.

Layering

This is an ideal method for ground-cover roses with trailing stems, but layering can also be used for any

USING LAYERING FOR PROPAGATING

1 Choose a healthy, well-ripened shoot and carefully bend down the selected stem to ground level. If damaged, cut off the tip first, down to the next strong bud.

2 About 20–25cm (8–10in) back from the stem end, make a dip in the soil, with a sloping side nearest the parent plant and a vertical side furthest away.

rose with stems that are long and flexible enough to be bent over to ground level.

After flowering in summer, take a strong, healthy, well-ripened shoot and bend it down to ground level. About 20–25cm (8–10in) back from the shoot tip, make a depression in the soil, 5–8cm (2–3in) deep, with a sloping side nearest the parent plant and an almost vertical side furthest away. Remove the leaves to create a clear length of stem above the shallow depression, and peg this down into the hole using a wooden peg or a bent U-shaped piece of wire.

Make sure that the section to be buried has at least one leaf joint or node, since it is from here that roots are most readily produced. The shoot tip should lie up against the almost vertical side of the depression in the soil, so that you get a good bend in the stem, and needs to be supported in an upright position by tying it to a split cane.

Backfill the hole with soil, firm in gently, and water well. The stem should have produced roots by the following spring, when it can be separated from the parent plant by severing the connecting stem.

The new stem can then be lifted, with its own root system intact, and transferred to another flowering site.

An alternative, more traditional technique involves 'wounding' the stem by cutting a 2.5cm (1in) long, shallow slit on its underside and pegging this open with a spent matchstick before pegging it down into the hole. But, providing you get a good bend on the stem, a bent stem will root almost as readily as a wounded stem. It will also not have the risk of fungal diseases or other pathogens entering the wound site, which may cause the layering to fail.

3 Lightly cultivate the base of the 5–8cm (2–3in) deep depression, and incorporate a little grit into the soil to improve the drainage.

4 Remove the leaves from the portion of stem to be buried, and place it in the prepared depression. Bend the stem end upwards against the vertical side.

5 Peg the stem into the base of the depression with a wooden peg or piece of bent wire, and backfill with soil. Secure the stem upright using a split cane.

Pruning

The main time for pruning is during the dormant season, between late autumn and early spring; in very cold climates, however, pruning is best delayed until early spring.

Ground-cover roses need little pruning on planting other than to remove dead, damaged, diseased or weak growth. Miniature, Patio and Polyantha roses are cut back hard on planting, to about 8–15cm (3–6in) above ground level for Patio and Polyantha roses, and to 5–8cm (2–3in) for miniatures. Cut back each strong shoot to a healthy, outward-facing bud. Remove completely weak or spindly shoots and any that are dead or damaged.

Once established, trailing ground-cover roses need pruning only to keep them within bounds, by cutting back overlong shoots to an upward-facing bud. Do this for once-flowering roses after flowering and for repeat-flowerers when dormant, in early spring. For the shrubby ground-cover roses, prune back the tips of over-long stems lightly and, if the bush is overcrowded, shorten sideshoots to two or three buds from their base.

Prune established miniature, Patio and Polyantha roses in early spring. Remove dead, diseased and damaged wood and any weak, spindly shoots,

PRUNING ROSES

1 Always use clean, sharp secateurs (pruners) and cut to a strong bud. Make a sloping cut that is angled away from the bud, with the lower end of the cut about 6mm (¼in) above the bud.

2 When pruning newly planted roses, the aim is to remove any weak ones at the base and cut back strong stems to an outward-facing bud, so that they grow out to create a light, airy, open centre.

then take out any that cross each other or the centre of the bush by cutting back to their point of origin. This is often sufficient to maintain good flowering, but if the rose has not thrived in the previous season, shorten the remaining shoots by up to two-thirds of their length, cutting back to a strong, outward-facing bud.

Miniature climbers

Climbers need no pruning in their first two or three growing seasons, other than to remove or shorten weak shoots. It is important in the early years to guide and tie in young shoots

to their support when still young and flexible. Tie shoots as near to the horizontal as possible, fanning them out across the support to provide full cover, as this improves flowering. If the rose is slow to branch, prune the tips of main shoots back by about 5cm (2in) to a strong bud. Once established, in early spring, remove dead, weak and unhealthy growth, and shorten flowered shoots by two-thirds of their length, cutting to a strong bud. As the rose matures, any less productive shoots can be cut back to the base; this should stimulate new replacement shoots that can be tied in to fill any gaps in the cover.

Calendar

Early winter

Plant bare-root and containerized miniature roses when weather conditions are favourable.

Mid-winter

Peruse catalogues for last-minute orders. Plant bare-root or containerized roses in periods of good weather, when soil is not waterlogged, dry or frozen. Apply a tar-oil winter wash, if desired, to reduce the need for fungicide sprays later in the season. Check hardwood cuttings regularly, and re-firm if lifted by frost. In mild winter climates, finish pruning repeat-flowering roses. Improve soil for new plantings in spring by incorporating organic matter.

Late winter

Plant roses that were ordered earlier in winter, or heel them in, if necessary, until conditions improve.

Early spring

Plant containerized roses; last chance for planting bare-root roses. Apply a 5–8cm (2–3in) layer of mulch at the base of established plants. Apply fertilizer as new growth begins to emerge. Prune repeat-flowering roses in regions with very cold winters.

Mid- to late spring

Continue planting containerized stock; keep watered until established. Apply preventative fungicide as leaves emerge. Check for and treat aphids, blackspot and leaf-rolling sawfly.

Summer

Tie in new shoots of climbers throughout the growing season. Feed all roses after the first flush of flowers. Water roses in open ground, if necessary, when hot, dry weather is prolonged. Water all container-grown roses regularly and feed with liquid fertilizer. Check for and control aphids, powdery mildew, blackspot and rust. Deadhead repeat-flowering roses. Deadhead once-flowering roses, unless you want the hips, and prune, if necessary, after flowering. Take semi-ripe cuttings in mid- to late summer. Layer trailing roses after flowering. Visit gardens, peruse new specialist catalogues, and plan for autumn ordering of roses, especially those that may be less readily available in local garden centres.

Early autumn

Place orders for roses from specialist catalogues. Apply high potash fertilizer to roses that are not growing well. Take hardwood cuttings.

Mid- to late autumn

In climates with a mild winter only, begin pruning repeat-flowering roses. Tie in climbing roses, to secure them against winter gales. Dig over and improve soil, ready for new plantings. Begin planting bare-root roses; the planting season extends to early spring during periods when the soil is not too wet, dry or frozen. Rake up and burn fallen rose leaves.

■ ABOVE
In summer, tie in the shoots of climbers while they are still young and flexible.

Pests and diseases

A list of pests and diseases gives a sense of foreboding, as if rose growing always entails a constant battle against the ravages of nature. Below are the most common afflictions, but with the improved disease-resistance of modern roses, you may suffer only one or two of them, and with prompt action, you will avoid great problems.

Aphids

Identification: Small, green or pink sap-sucking insects, usually clustered at the shoot tips and on flower buds. They cause stunting and distortion of growth and may transmit viruses.
Control: Easily controlled if treated promptly. A specific aphicide containing pirimicarb will not harm beneficial insects such as lacewings and ladybirds. Organic gardeners can remove by hand, using gloves, or use soft soap, derris or pyrethrum.

Balling

Identification: Flowers have a slack appearance, petals are brown and fail to open properly. Caused by prolonged wet weather, or rain followed by hot sun; some roses are more susceptible than others. The disorder alone does not affect the long-term health of the rose, but if balled flowers become infected with fungi, dieback may occur.
Control: Deadhead promptly, by cutting back to a healthy bud or leaf.

Blackspot

Identification: A fungal disease causing black spots on the leaves (sometimes also on the stems) followed by yellowing and, in severe cases, defoliation, badly weakening the plant.

Control: Treat with a fungicide just after spring pruning, and repeat according to the manufacturer's instructions. Remove and burn all affected foliage promptly. Rake up and burn any fallen leaves in autumn, and apply a tar-oil winter wash.

Dieback

Identification: Stems discolour and die back from the tips, and take on a characteristic dry, tan-brown appearance. Flower buds may wither. May be caused by fungal infections that gain entry via pruning wounds, by cold damage, poor growing conditions, or nutrient deficiencies, especially of potash and phosphorus.
Control: Cut out all affected wood back to a bud on clean, healthy wood (the pith will be white with no sign of brown staining).

■ ABOVE RIGHT
Dieback affects stem tips first, then progresses down the stem.

■ RIGHT
The early stages of blackspot. Preventative measures and good hygiene help to reduce the incidence of this disease.

■ RIGHT
Aphids cluster at shoot tips and on other soft tissues that are easily pierced by their mouthparts.

systemic insecticide. You will not reverse damage already caused, but you will reduce emerging populations that lay their eggs in subsequent years. If you have had this problem one year, you can expect it the next; you can achieve some protection by spraying the undersides of the leaves with insecticide in late spring or very early summer, before adults lay eggs.

Control: Ensure roses have adequate moisture by mulching well and watering in prolonged dry periods. Prune out affected shoots and treat the remainder with a fungicidal spray.

Leaf-cutting bees

Identification: Neat, semicircular or circular holes are cut out from the leaf margins; the bees use them to make nests for their young. Damage is largely cosmetic and will not affect the health of established plants.
Control: If damage is severe, carefully disturb the insects using a fly swat; bees are beneficial pollinators and do not justify the use of chemicals.

Leaf-rolling sawfly

Identification: In late spring or early summer, rose leaflets become tightly rolled around freshly laid eggs; the caterpillar eats the leaves as it emerges.
Control: At the leaf-rolling stage, leaves can be picked off if infestation is light. For more severe attacks, leave the foliage in place and spray with a

Powdery mildew

Identification: White or greyish white powdery fungal growth appears on upper leaf surfaces or on both surfaces of young leaves; affected leaves may drop prematurely. May also affect stems and flower buds. Prevalent where soil is dry and air is moist and stagnant; often affects wall-grown roses, where air circulation is poor and soil is dry at the foot of the wall.

Rust

Identification: Orange spots appear on leaf stalks and leaf surfaces in early summer with orange pustules on the leaf undersides and, later in summer, pustules that contain overwintering spores. Leaves may drop prematurely.
Control: Spores are spread by wind and rain splash, and need damp, humid conditions to thrive. Do not plant roses too closely, and keep bushes open-centred for good air circulation. Prune out infected stems in spring; burn prunings promptly. Spray with a suitable fungicide.

■ ABOVE LEFT
Rose rust appears as orange spots on leaf stalks, and surfaces in early summer.

■ LEFT
Neatly notched leaves indicate the activities of leaf-cutting bees.

Other recommended roses

'**Anna Livia**' (**syn.** '**Kormetter**', '**Trier 2000**') A compact Floribunda with broad, well-filled sprays of rounded, sweetly scented, clear pink flowers from summer to autumn. 75 x 60cm (30 x 24in).

'**Arizona Sunset**' A miniature of dense, bushy habit, with clusters of small, cupped, pale yellow flowers, flushed with orange-red, throughout summer to autumn. The flowers are good for cutting, and this little rose is often grown for exhibition. 40 x 30cm (16 x 12in).

'**Baby Masquerade**' (**syn.** '**Baby Carnival**') A miniature bush with many small, double, rosette-shaped flowers borne in clusters from summer to autumn. The petals are yellow, flushed with pink and red. Ideal for containers and low edging. 40 x 40cm (16 x 16in).

'**Bit o' Sunshine**' A miniature bush rose that is reliably floriferous, it bears masses of small, double, rather flat, pale yellow flowers from summer to autumn. Ideal for containers of all types, and for border edging. 30 x 30cm (12 x 12in).

'**Bonica**' (**syn.** '**Bonica '82**', '**Meidomonac**') An award-winning compact bush rose with glossy foliage, freely producing large clusters of

'Baby Masquerade'

double, lightly scented, rose-pink flowers from summer to autumn. A perfect specimen for small gardens, it is also useful for beds, borders and low hedging. 90cm x 1.1m (3 x 3½ft).

'**Chatsworth**' (**syn.** '**Mirato**', '**Tanotari**', '**Tanotax**') A spreading ground-cover rose with dense, fresh green foliage and many small, double, cupped flowers of deep rich pink, borne in broad clusters from summer to autumn. Good for sunny banks and containers (including large hanging baskets), and also available as a standard. 60cm x 1.1m (2 x 3½ft).

'**Climbing Pompon de Paris**' A China rose of daintily arching growth, producing a single, early summer flush of many small, double button-like blooms of rich rose-red, in admirable contrast to the grey-green leaves. The flexible

'Bit o' Sunshine'

stems are easily trained horizontally on a wall, or can be allowed to scramble along the ground. 3.5 x 2.5m (11 x 8ft).

'**Colibre '79**' (**syn.** '**Colibre '80**'; '**Medianover**') A miniature bush rose with clusters of cupped, double flowers of unusual colouring – the orange-yellow ground colour is heavily veined with deep red-pink – that are produced freely from summer to autumn. Ideal for window boxes and other small containers. 30 x 30cm (12 x 12in).

'**De Meaux**' (**syn.** *Rosa centifolia* var. *pomponia*) A charming little Centifolia rose of twiggy habit, producing tiny, nicely scented pompon flowers of beautiful clear pink, each no more than 2.5cm (1in) across, in mid-summer. Dating back to 1789, this diminutive rose has the

'Bonica'

typical scent and colour of the Old Roses. It is perfect for containers and pots, and as edging at the front of a mixed bed or border. 60 x 75cm (24 x 30in).

'**Dearest**' A compact bush rose producing large clusters of rounded, soft rose-pink blooms with attractive wavy petals, from summer to autumn. Excellent for low hedging, beds and containers. 60 x 60cm (24 x 24in).

'**Dresden Doll**' A modern miniature rose of very old-fashioned appearance, with mossy glandular growth on the buds and stems, much like the old Moss roses. The scented flowers are cupped, fully double, and of a beautiful shade of soft shell-pink; unlike Moss roses, it repeats well from summer to autumn. Ideal for window boxes and troughs. 25 x 15cm (10 x 6in).

'Colibre '79'

'Essex'

'Gentle Touch'

'Drummer Boy' (syn. 'Harvacity') A strong and healthy Patio rose of bushy habit, bearing dense clusters of many small, semi-double flowers with frilled petals of deep red above dark, glossy foliage. Perfect for containers and low hedging. 40 x 45cm (16 x 18in).

'Essex' (syn. 'Pink Cover', 'Poulnoz') A creeping ground-cover rose of dense habit, with glossy, dark green foliage. The long stems are wreathed throughout summer and into autumn with sprays of small, single, star-like blooms of rich pink with white centres. Good for clothing sunny and inaccessible banks, or for cascading over the tops of retaining walls and trellises; it can also be grown in hanging baskets. One of the English 'County' series. 60cm x 1.2m (2 x 4ft).

'Fairyland' (syn. 'Harlayalong') This Polyantha shrub of low, sprawling habit is often included among the ground-cover roses. It has abundant small, glossy leaves and produces cupped, fully double, rosette-shaped flowers of soft pink in trusses from summer to autumn. Ideal for tall containers. 60cm x 1.2m (2 x 4ft).

'Fire Princess' A miniature bush of upright habit, with small, double rosette, vibrant orange blooms that glow above dark foliage. 45 x 40cm (18 x 16in).

'Gentle Touch' (syn. 'Diclulu') A Patio rose of dense, neat habit, bearing clusters of lightly scented, perfectly urn-shaped, semi-double flowers of softest pale pink just above the dark, glossy foliage, from summer to autumn. Excellent for low hedging and

containers, and the flowers are irresistible for cutting. 40 x 40cm (16 x 16in).

'Gingernut' (syn. 'Coccrazy') A compact, bushy Patio rose with glossy foliage and dense clusters of cupped, orange-bronze flowers overlaid with red and pink, borne from summer to autumn. Suitable for containers, low hedging and bedding. 40 x 45cm (16 x 18in).

'Good as Gold' (syn. 'Chewsunbeam') A miniature climber with clusters of double, rich yellow flowers with pointed petals that open from urn-shaped buds in almost continuous succession from summer to autumn. It has a good scent and would be perfect over an entrance way. 2 x 1.5m (6 x 5ft).

'Grouse' (syn. 'Immensee', 'Korimro', 'Lac Rose') A trailing ground-cover shrub forming mounds of small,

very shiny leaves with long, flexible stems. Bears small, single, flat flowers of blush-pink with a boss of golden stamens at their centre. Flowers once in summer. Excellent for covering fairly large areas of sunny bank. 60cm x 3m (2 x 10ft).

'Hotline' (syn. 'Aromikeh') A miniature bush with mossy buds and stems, bearing high-pointed, semi-double red flowers from summer to autumn. 45 x 35cm (18 x 14in).

'Jeanne Lajoie' A miniature climber with dark, glossy foliage and fully double, high-pointed flowers of soft lavender-pink borne from summer to autumn. 2m x 70cm (6ft x 28in).

'Katharina Zeimet' A very pretty dwarf Polyantha with dark foliage and delicate sprays of many small, double, cupped, sweetly scented white flowers borne almost continuously from summer to autumn. An ideal plant for containers. 50 x 50cm (20 x 20in).

'Laura Ashley' A dense, free-flowering ground-cover rose with profuse clusters of many small, single, slightly cupped magenta to lilac-pink flowers with a sweet fragrance, produced from summer to autumn. 60cm x 1.2m (2 x 4ft).

'**Little Bo-peep**' (**syn.** '**Poullen**') A Patio rose with a dense, low-spreading habit that is also used as ground cover for confined spaces. It has dense clusters of small, semi-double, rather flattened, palest pink flowers from summer to autumn. 30 x 50cm (12 x 20in).

'**Little Flirt**' A colourful and compact miniature bush rose of neat, upright habit, producing small, double blooms, opening from buds of brilliant pink with a paler pink petal reverse; the colour fades quickly in strong sunlight. Ideal for containers and window boxes. 40 x 25cm (16 x 10in).

'**Little Rambler**' (**syn.** '**Chewramb**') A petite rambling rose with well-filled clusters of small, fully double rosette-shaped flowers of soft pink, produced from summer to autumn – a long flowering period for a rambler. Use for fences, trellis work, pillars or for scrambling in shrubs. 2.2 x 2.2m (7 x 7ft).

'**Magic Carousel**' A miniature bush with glossy foliage and, from summer to autumn, small, pale yellow, rosette-shaped flowers with crimson petal margins. A cheerful little bush for containers, window boxes or low edging. 40 x 30cm (16 x 12in).

'Little Flirt'

'**Nozomi**' (**syn.** '**Heideröslein**') A once-flowering ground-cover rose with trailing stems and many small, single, starry blooms of soft blush-pink; occasionally produces a second flush of flowers in late summer. A small rose that works well in the rock garden. 45cm x 1.2m (18in x 4ft).

'**Partridge**' (**syn.** '**Korweirim**', '**Lac Blanc**', '**Weisse Immensee**') This vigorous ground-cover rose is prostrate, creeping a few inches above ground, but with considerable spread. The mounds of small, glossy, dark green leaves are almost obscured in mid-summer with the sprays of small, single, slightly cupped, sweetly scented white flowers. Effective on sunny banks and as a low ribbon edging at the front of a border. 60cm x 3m (2 x 10ft).

'Partridge'

'**Party Girl**' A bushy miniature rose with fragrant, beautifully formed, high-centred flowers of apricot-yellow flushed with salmon-pink, borne from summer to autumn. Often grown for exhibition and very pretty as a houseplant, provided it has excellent light. 35 x 35cm (14 x 14in).

'**Petite de Hollande**' (**syn.** '**Normandica**', Petit Junon de Hollande', '**Pompon des Dames**') A small, bushy, old-fashioned Centifolia rose flowering once in summer. The clusters of small, sweetly scented, double, pompon-like flowers are rose-pink with darker pink centres. Perfect for containers of classical style. 1 x 1m (3 x 3ft).

'**Pheasant**' (**syn.** '**Heidekönigin**', '**Kordapt**', '**Palissade Rose**') A creeping ground-cover rose with dense foliage and long stems

'Pink Chimo'

wreathed in cupped, double pale pink flowers, with golden stamens; blooms once only in mid-summer. Good as ground cover for extensive areas. 50cm x 3m (20in x 10ft).

'**Pink Bells**' (**syn.** '**Poulbells**') Dense, spreading ground-cover rose with abundant glossy foliage and long stems bearing many clusters of small, double, bright pink pompon blooms, flowering once only in mid-summer. Good for sunny banks, cascading over walls and for tall containers. 75cm x 1.5m (30in x 5ft).

'**Pink Chimo**' (**syn.** '**Interchimp**') A tough ground-cover shrub with ample, leathery foliage and cupped, semi-double, deep pink flowers wreathing the stems from summer to autumn. Makes an attractive plant in tall containers or large hanging baskets. 60 x 90cm (2 x 3ft).

'Pink Meidiland'

'Stacey Sue'

'Viridiflora'

'Pink Meidiland' (**syn.** 'Meipoque') A ground-cover rose of dense, compact habit, flowering continuously from summer to autumn. The attractive, relatively large, single, cupped, bright carmine-pink flowers with white centres and golden stamens are borne in clusters. It is suitable for the middle ranks of a shrub or mixed border, for massed plantings, and for low hedging. 1.1m x 75cm (3½ft x 30in).

'Red Blanket' (**syn.** 'Intercell') A dense ground-cover shrub with dense, dark foliage and clusters of well-formed, flat, semi-double flowers that are pale pink at the centre, shading to deeper pink and red-pink at the margins. Blooms from summer to autumn. Excellent in tall containers, sunny banks and for the tops of walls. 75cm x 1.2m (30in x 4ft).

'Roulettii' (**syn.** *Rosa chinensis* var. *minima*, **'Pompon de Paris'**) A diminutive, free-flowering China rose with tiny, matt, dark green leaflets and double, deep rose-pink, cupped flowers produced singly and in small airy clusters from summer to autumn. Perfect for window boxes and other containers. 20 x 20cm (8 x 8in).

'Sneezy' A diminutive Polyantha rose, this healthy little bush is perfect for smaller containers, troughs and especially window boxes. Ideal for the smallest of gardens or on a terrace or balcony, it produces masses of single pink flowers from summer to autumn. 30 x 30cm (12 x 12in).

'Snow Carpet' (**syn.** 'Maccarpe') A low, creeping miniature ground-cover rose with shiny, bright green

foliage and fully double, creamy white pompon flowers produced over a long period in mid-summer. Excellent for hanging baskets and other containers. 15 x 45cm (6 x 18in).

'Sophie's Perpetual' (**syn.** 'Dresden China') An almost thornless China rose that can be used as a small climber; it bears clusters of well-scented, almost globular, semi-double flowers of blush-pink clusters, overlaid with deep pink cerise. Flowers almost continuously from summer to autumn. 2.5 x 1.2m (8 x 4ft).

'Spong' A small Centifolia rose producing small, beautifully formed, rounded, almost pompon-like, rose-pink flowers above abundant greyish-green foliage in mid-summer. Excellent for containers (it was bred in 1805 and recommended then for

this purpose) and for the front of mixed borders. 1.2m x 90cm (4 x 3ft).

'Stacey Sue' An award-winning miniature bush bearing well-filled sprays of small, pink, rosette-shaped flowers from summer to autumn above neat, glossy foliage. It looks exquisite in terracotta containers, and particularly lovely in window boxes or troughs on a balcony. 25 x 30cm (10 x 12in).

'The Valois Rose' (**syn.** 'Kordadel') An exceptionally pretty Patio rose with dark foliage and clusters of lightly scented, creamy yellow, rounded flowers shaded with carmine at the petal margins, produced from summer to autumn. Perfect as a specimen plant in containers, as low edging or at the front of a mixed border. 40 x 30cm (16 x 12in).

'Viridiflora' This compact little bush makes an interesting specimen and, although loved by flower arrangers, is curious rather than truly beautiful. The small, double, purple-tinged green, rounded flowers are made up of modified leaves rather than true petals; it flowers freely from summer to autumn. Grow in a mixed border or rose bed. 75 x 60cm (30 x 24in).

Index

aphids, 41, 51, 58

balling, 58
blackspot, 41, 51, 58
bush roses, 19
buying miniature roses, 40–1

Centifolia roses, 9, 15, 18
China roses, 9, 10, 11, 15
classification, 18–19
climbers, 16, 19, 56
colours, 45
containers, 46–7, 50–1
cut flowers, 17
cuttings, 52–4

deadheading, 41, 51
dieback, 58
diseases, 41, 51, 58–9

fertilizers, 43, 49, 51
flowers, 18, 19
fungal diseases, 51

ground-cover roses, 9, 11, 14–15,
   19, 49, 54–5, 56

hanging baskets, 48
houseplants, 17

landscaping fabric, 49
layering, 54–5
leaf-cutting bees, 59
leaf-rolling sawfly, 59

mildew, powdery, 59
Miniature roses, 12–13, 56
mulches, 43, 49, 50

Old Garden roses, 18

Patio roses, 9, 11, 12, 13–14, 18, 56
pegging down, 49, 55
pests, 41, 51, 58–9
planting roses, 42–3, 44–8
Polyantha roses, 9 10–11, 15, 18, 56
propagation, 52–3
pruning, 56

Rosa 'Angela Rippon', 20
   R. 'Anna Ford', 20
   R. 'Anna Livia', 60
   R. 'Apricot Summer', 21

R. 'Arizona Sunset', 60
R. 'Avon', 21
R. 'Baby Love', 21
R. 'Baby Masquerade', 60
R. 'Ballerina', 22
R. 'Bit o' Sunshine', 60
R. 'Bonica', 60
R. 'Broadlands', 22
R. canina, 9
R. 'Captain Scarlet', 22
R. 'Cécile Brünner', 15, 41
R. 'Chatsworth', 60
R. chinensis, 10, 11, 18
R. 'Cider Cup', 23
R. 'City Lights', 23
R. 'Climbing Iceberg', 14
R. 'Climbing Orange Sunblaze', 24
R. 'Climbing Pompon de Paris', 60
R. 'Colibre '79', 60
R. 'Conservation', 24
R. 'Crimson Gem', 25
R. 'Darling Flame', 25
R. 'De Meaux', 18, 60
R. 'Dearest', 60
R. 'Dresden Doll', 60
R. 'Drummer Boy', 61
R. 'Essex', 61
R. 'Fairyland', 61
R. 'Festival', 25
R. 'Fire Princess', 61
R. 'Fresh Pink', 26
R. 'Gentle Touch', 61

R. 'Gingernut', 61
R. 'Gloria Mundi', 26
R. 'Good as Gold', 61
R. 'Grouse', 61
R. 'Hakuun', 27
R. 'Hampshire', 27
R. 'Hotline', 61
R. 'Indian Sunblaze', 27
R. 'Jean Lajoie', 61
R. 'Katharina Zeimet', 61
R. 'Kent', 28
R. 'Lady Penelope', 29
R. 'Laura Ashley', 14, 61
R. 'Laura Ford', 28
R. 'Little Bo-Peep', 62
R. 'Little Flirt', 62
R. 'Little Rambler', 62
R. 'Little White Pet', 6, 29
R. 'Magic Carousel', 62
R. 'Mini Metro', 29
R. 'Mr Bluebird', 30
R. 'Nice Day', 30
R. 'Northamptonshire', 31
R. 'Nozomi', 14, 62
R. 'Old Blush', 10
R. 'Orange Sunblaze', 31
R. 'Oranges and Lemons', 31
R. 'Oxfordshire', 32
R. 'Partridge', 62
R. 'Party Girl', 62
R. 'Peace', 9
R. 'Peek a Boo', 32

R. 'Perle d'Or', 15, 32
R. 'Petite de Hollande' 18, 62
R. 'Pheasant', 62
R. 'Pink Bells', 62
R. 'Pink Chimo', 62
R. 'Pink Meidiland', 63
R. 'Pretty Polly', 33
R. 'Queen Mother', 33, 43
R. 'Red Ace', 34
R. 'Red Blanket', 63
R. 'Red Meidiland', 34
R. 'Rise 'n' Shine', 35
R. 'Roulettii', 10, 11, 12, 63
R. roxburghii, 9
R. 'Scarlet Meidiland', 35
R. 'Sneezy', 63
R. 'Snow Carpet', 63
R. 'Sophie's Perpetual', 63
R. 'Spong', 63
R. 'Stacey Sue', 63
R. 'Sun Hit', 35
R. 'Surrey', 36
R. 'Sussex', 36
R. 'Swany', 36
R. 'Sweet Dream', 37
R. 'Sweet Magic', 37
R. 'The Fairy', 38
R. 'The Valois Rose', 63
R. 'Top Marks', 38, 47
R. 'Viridiflora', 63
R. 'Warm Welcome', 38
R. 'White Cécile Brünner', 39
R. 'White Flower Carpet', 11, 39
R. 'Wiltshire', 39
R. 'Yellow Flower Carpet', 8

rose soil sickness, 42
rust, 41, 59

soil, 42–3

watering, 48, 50
weeds, 43, 50
wild roses, 18
wind damage, 42

■ RIGHT
'Queen Mother'.

ACKNOWLEDGEMENTS
All pictures were taken by
Peter Anderson, with the
exception of the following:
A–Z Botanical Collection 8–9b,
10t; John Freeman 8bc, 16b;
Michelle Garrett 17tl, 17tr; 17b;
Harry Smith Collection 8l, 11,
13, 16t; Peter McHoy 61r.